AS GOOD AS SALT

Elizabeth Bewick

PETERLOO POETS

First published in 2006
by Peterloo Poets
The Old Chapel, Sand Lane, Calstock,
Cornwall PL18 9QX, U.K.
© 2006 by Elizabeth Bewick

A catalogue record for this book is available
from the British Library

ISBN 1-904324-33-9

Printed in Great Britain by
Antony Rowe Ltd, Chippenham, Wilts.

ACKNOWLEDGEMENTS

Acknowledgements are due to the editors of *South* magazine in which some of these poems first appeared, also to Graham Williams of the Florin Press, who published some of the love poems in my first book, *Comfort Me With Apples*, illustrated with his own line wood engravings and with an introduction by Kevin Crossley-Holland.

'Chagall Window' first appeared in *The Otter Memorial Papers*, No 14, edited by Paul Foster at University College, Chichester, and 'Oranges at Christmas Time' in *Light Unlocked: Christmas Card Poems*, edited by Kevin Crossley-Holland and Lawrence Sail, published by Enitharmon Press.

'House of Girls' is unashamedly reprinted from my second Peterloo volume, *Making a Roux*; it seemed to belong with the earlier love poems.

Most of all I owe my thanks to my friends, especially to Kay and all the members of our workshop, without whose help and support I could not have enjoyed writing in my eighties or be looking forward with continued interest and curiosity to my nineties!

This book is for my friends
with my love and thanks

My friends have been like daily bread
Essential yet unmerited:
As kind as sunshine after rain
Or firelight on the window pane:
As kind as harbour lights at sea
Or some familiar melody:
As good as salt my friends to me.

(Anon)

CONTENTS

Love Songs Grave and Gay

1.

An anodyne, you said, but now I find
that all my tenderness has been in vain
to smooth the jagged corners of your mind
or ease the tension in your furrowed brain;
you groan aloud and panic grips me tight
twisting my stomach in a sudden pain:
what use is love, if it can shed no light
to point your way to sanity again.

2.

We measure love when we are very young
with anxious probings: how much and how long?
Do you love me as well as I love you
and will you love me for one year, or two? –
seeking as children to conceal in rhyme
that what we mean is to the end of time.

We measure time when we are growing old,
knowing that measured love is love grown cold,
with backward glances at the hell and heaven
of love withheld as well as freely given,
seeking lost childhood and the right to choose
once more the path we hoped our feet could use;
the how much and how long now turned to fear
of losing everything we hold most dear.

3.

Hug-a-hug-hug
three men on a jug,
how nice to be me
to have them all three,
to change now and then
at the stroke of a pen,
to turn them around
and say – 'Look what I've found'
and knock them all flat,
if I feel just like that.
Hug-a-hug-glee,
how nice to be me!

4.

Mother you,
smother you,
wrap you in silk –
what shall I do
if you don't want hot milk?

Chatter
and natter,
not let you just think –
what shall I do
if it drives you to drink?

Shall I moan,
shall I groan,
shall I shriek to the sky
that if you don't love me
I lie down and die?

Oh no, my sweet poet,
I'm not yet so old
that I can't take another lamb
in from the cold!

5.

Swathed in the lapping silk
of Badedas-scented water –
foaming like ass's milk –
a Cleopatra's daughter,
content to dream away
the time that should be spent
in planning of my day
with purposeful intent,
I lie and think of you
in sensuous delight,
as green Badedas dew
dispels the shades of night.

6.

By mock blue flames of fire
I sat and watched the play
of sad and mad desire
and haunting birds of prey.

Each scene, each gesture made
with beautiful precision,
so elegantly played
in decorous decision.

So near you were, my dear,
I watched your face throughout,
untroubled by the fear
of day's succeeding doubt.

Mind linked with kindred mind,
no need a word to speak:
I know that I shall find you
here again next week!

7.

Hope rises in my heart
to leaven in my brain,
and happiness like froth
works in my head again.

Bread should be risen twice
like any lovers oath,
but if knocked back too hard
will never make a loaf.

For you I'll work the yeast
into the lightest dough,
fit for a royal feast
that only you will know.

And on each crusty slice
of heaven new-baked each day
you'll spread fresh butter thick
and eat it your own way.

8.

You home in on the sun
as swallows flying south,
finding the warmth you need
upon my willing mouth,
knowing, wild bird, at last
however far you roam,
each flight from winter's cold
will bring you nearer home.

9.

I love my love with an R
because he is the rind
of all the apples in the world
that dance along my mind,
that dance along the wind
and fall from off the tree
into the cupped and loving hands
still waiting there for me.

I love my love with a G
because he is the green
of all the apples in the world
still ripening on the tree,
soon red as my heart's red blood
for all the world to see
and sweeter all the more
from waiting there for me.

Roundelay

Purple sheets
that trap the night
closely in a dark delight;
dragonflies that dart in flight
through the whispers of the night;

lovers
bedding in delight
whisper closely through the night
secrets caught
like joy in flight:

purple spread of night's delight.

My Heart under your Hand

What is this door
you say I close,
to leave you standing
cold and fearful
in the dark?

There is no door
that will not yield
to your demanding,
nor one to which
I have not given you the key.

My heart waits
to lie safe under your hand,
my face is turned
towards the light of day,
you need but step
into my threshold's trust,
no path to find,
no door to bar the way.

The Herb Woman

Perhaps you feed on worry, thrive on pain,
react more keenly under strong duress;
better perhaps to leave you comfortless –
stretched out on tenterhooks at breaking strain –
than proffer healing comfort of my own,
pouring love's balm into an open sore
where it can only serve to sting the more
until new skin above the hurt has grown.

Time, the great healer, so the sages tell
will bring you comfort better than my store
of simple herbs, but should you shun its light –
locked by despair within your private hell –
I find a way to batter down the door
and share with you that everlasting night.

Sahara Dust

It did not need
a newsreader to say
brown dust had fallen
in the region of my heart,
but that it should be hot,
from the Sahara blown seemed strange.
They should be
chilling winds
not hot
that blow such words
as heart and mind
this morning tried
painfully to assimilate.

Or is that heat
part of the irony
of which our love-each-other
is compounded?
First sweet, then bitter,
sweet and yet again
thrown back to bitterness,
unable to be set
in any mould for long;
like my attempts at making marmalade
which would not gel
though boiled and boiled again
till, anxious for results,
I added lemon gelatine
certain to make it set,
but certain too
to spoil the freshness
of ingredients.

But not for you I made
the bitter-sweet of marmalade;
for you there'll always be
a store of natural honey
waiting to be spread
upon my home-baked bread,
honey so pure and rare
you will not even care
how long it has been stored,
in heart of oak matured,
or mellowed by the years
of my too-certain tears.

Secrets

The quality of kinship,
which you name as near to incest, binds us without shame
so close together as to whisper bold
secrets not given voice before,
nor told to other living soul by word or deed,
though in the telling now our minds are freed
from childhood manacles of biting steel,
only to forge a closer link to feel
and fetter thought, if you would have it so.

No, rather let us freely think and go
our separate ways, our separate paths to find
to that elusive garden of the mind
where early snowdrops and fast-spreading weed
together grow, arid common efforts lead
towards the digging of a deeper grave
for all things rank, the purer flowers to save
to scent the air with sweetness and to spread
the virgin sheets of our most common bed.

Heartbreak

O, hearts don't break,
they merely ache,
a blue-black bruise,
a shameful ooze of soggy sentiment,
and grit of sediment
to twist the gut
with if and but
and wring the last
tear from the past;
obsessive in self-pity's pain:
no break to make-and-mend again.

Love's Ransom

Is this what a few pence could do for you?
buy you an hour or so of unfraught time
in which to think and exercise anew
your mastery of words in well-wrought rhyme,
trim your taut rhythms and your metre both
to verse that makes an impact on the mind,
hacking your way through rolling undergrowth
with shriek of mandrake root torn out, to find
again the snowdrops of the spring of youth,
when you first ran on bare feet wet with dew –
eyes wide with wonder in the dawn of truth
nights darkness only strength in sleep renewed –
if I could act as such a thief of time
gladly I'd pay a ransom for your rhyme.

Love's Rainbow

I fashioned a rainbow for your delight
fit for a dragonfly cover of night,
you set me weaving in battleship grey
squares for a coverlet heavy with day.

When daybreak came with no hint of light
or hope of a starlit singing night,
I sat there making my squares of grey,
the fourth fate weaving the world away.

And yet, if I heard your step so light
treading the path to our sure delight,
my dragonfly colours would oust the grey
and trap the night in a heart-long day.

The Wanton

I can be wanton should my lord demand
the unsleeved trick or two I've yet to play,
his wish has always been my loved command
and dalliance at dawn my longed-for day.
I can be gentle when his silken hair
falls all about my breasts in sated sleep,
my loving arms enclose him everywhere
as sanctuary should he need to weep.

I can be plain when his professional face
is turned to me in conversation's flow
and keep my admiration of his grace
well-disciplined so that it does not show.
All this I can, so long as I can tell
his kiss still reassures me I do well.

Love In A Cold Climate

1.

Today the sun shone weakly
after rain, and reading
(in the Observer Magazine)
of peaches, ripely grown,
soft-fleshed, white-skinned,
suddenly I remembered eating peaches with you.

Now I remember with delight
your frank appreciation
of ripe flesh, my own
child's innocence to woman grown;
your eyes my sun,
warm in my mouth
the fragrance of your fruit.

2.

We who spend our lives in a cold climate
blossom in the spring
like the fragile plants we have nursed
through the long winter.
Warm in the sun we grow in happiness
and tolerate the weeds
that pass for flowers in cottage gardens,
and the bluebell haze
swaying in the long grass we will not cut
until their blue is done.

Reflections of the long grass ripple
on my still pond,
I kneel beside it to admire the shrubs
of gravelled garden
that I thought would never grow;
I touch their leaves
with tentative and unskilled fingers
but in my heart
I touch your face, and happiness
spills over in the sun.

I cannot write a poem, she said

I cannot write a poem, she said,
with all these flowers in my head,
sunburst chrysanthemums and red
wine-splash red roses lately spread
on orange-blossom bridal bed,
I cannot write a poem, she said.

I cannot write a poem, she cried,
with so much bolstering my pride,
a squire closely by my side
to guide me through the forest ride
and push the bramble thorns aside.
I cannot write a poem, she cried.

I cannot write a poem, she said,
with red hot pokers in my bed
and all these flowers in my head,
with Richard waiting to be fed
on vintage wine and garlic bread,
I cannot write a poem, she said.

Cut-price Butterflies

Ridiculous to expect
cut-price butterflies
but I found them,
splendidly gold and purple
against the backdrop
of a sky-blue sheet,
and outside the moon
golden and full
within November's grey.

Twenty-four Hours Leave

How in one day
to play so many parts?

The housewife
baking in advance
brown bread, crisp apple tarts,
making your favourite jam.

Then, when I meet your coach,
excitement carefully controlled
but tingling nerve-ends in my feet
waiting to find if Cinderella's shoe
still fits.

Later the courtesan
and willing slave,
experienced lover
only in your arms,
wearing a padlocked chain of chastity
until you came
and teasing now
by testing it on you.

So much of life and love to cram
round-fisted in the rolling hours.

delights of bed and board
to hoard
against encroaching loneliness,
but never totally despair
nor pain of wanting,
you not there.

The walls alive with words
to ward off harm,
the imprint of your kiss
to keep me warm,
each night's defenceless dream
to hold you here –
each morning's waking light
brings next time near.

The Sea-Horse

My sea-horse,
sinuous and green,
has hung all day
upon my dress,
neither as god nor symbol seen
nor gold-eyed idol
to confess.

I lift its chain
above my head,
then stay my hand
from where it rests
and leave the weight,
not cold or dead,
to lie all night
between my breasts.

My sea-horse,
sinuous arid green,
in warmth and love
all night has lain;
I touch its weight,
unfelt, unseen,
and feel your hand
at rest again.

Misunderstanding

Sometimes
you take my words
and squeeze them thin,
then twist them round
to stab yourself
as if with a large pin
taken from my hand,
and I cringe
and want to cry
at the thought of the hurt
your words imply,
when I, God help me,
cannot hope to live
in any kind of peace
unless I give
you only love.

Plaint

You do not love me
I know you do not love me,
and yet your pressure on my hair is soft;
you do not heed me
I know you do not heed me,
and yet you listen gravely
when I say
that you should live your life some other way.

You do not love me
I know you do not love me,
and yet you seem contented with your lot;
you do not need me
I know you do not need me,
and yet you answer kindly
when I ask
what need you have that I should do some task.

You do not love me
I know you do not love me,
and yet I feel it in my very bones;
you do not love me
I know you do not love me,
but if this is not love that keeps us close
I can but say
I could not live my life some other way.

The Worm

No-one had given me a worm before:
the gift to end all gifts, my mind should sink
through sludging layers of thought to rotted core
of self-despair. Perhaps I should not shrink
from thoughts of worms and endings, neither crave
release from pain, though it uncoil the sweet
of ordered days, goose-shiver on my grave
and walk across my heart with day-cold feet.

A poet is a maker: now my hands
busy themselves with making, kneading bread
into fresh loaves of hope. My faith still stands
in obstinate derision of things dead:
within its resting dough the swaddled seed
lies cradled, ready for your springing need.

Seventy Not Out

After my seventieth birthday
we went to bed
and didn't get up again
for three days
except for more toast and tea
coffee, ham sandwiches
and the occasional pee

* * *

You stood up in the bath
and kissed me
through the curtain of your hair
its loose strands lying
like salt across my lips
and I was shaken
by the sound of the sea

House Of Girls

Beth is the shy one
still not sure of her profession –
I only keep her on
because she pleases you,
most demanding of my customers.

She welcomes you at the door,
fusses over you,
makes you feel important,
brings you brandy and coffee
to alleviate the stresses
of the day, the long drive here.

Lizzie runs your bath
softened with perfumed oils,
her skilful fingers
massage the tension from your body
till you sink deep in the waters.

Isabeau wakes you
running her fingers through your hair, arousing
with wasp-tongued kisses
the liquid passion on your lips,
soft in the unaccustomed morning.

But it is I, Elisavetta,
who am the Madam;
when you tire of my girls
I dismiss them to their cubicles
with a practised flick of my wrist.

It is I who wait on you
in the heat of the day,
until we neither know nor care
if it be noon or night,
day-break or sun-set
behind the close-drawn curtains.

I minister to your needs,
bringing more brandy and coffee,
smoked-salmon sandwiches,
and *Fanny by Gaslight*
which we read to each other in turn.

I take off my negligee
and the spray of orchids you gave me,
my grandparent's photographs
in the gold locket I always wear
nestling incongruously
between my naked breasts.

Only I have a key to this room –
the girls are not allowed –
but we both know
that when another morning comes
it is Beth who will send you back.

The Language of Skin

Our loving has no need to find a voice
the skin can speak a language of its own,
no words but moving subtleties of tone
in changing emphasis of mutual choice;
the rhythm of the blood proclaims the tune
for hammered hearts to drum with mounting pride,
crescendos of ascending notes provide
fresh meaning to love's ancient bardic rune.

Your reaching hands unfold my body's trust
revealing layered petals of my lust
until you reach the centre of my art,
your music interweaves its notes with mine,
I tap my riddles on your curving spine
and hold your withered flower to my heart.

Untitled

Richard, when I see your body, slim
    and naked on my bed
        my senses dim
            and words remain unsaid.

Can you still see in me at seventy
    more than the fat old woman that I am,
        or do you feel a warmth, serenity
            beyond the span of time?

When resting between my milkless breasts, you find
    comfort at last for your so-troubled mind,
        then you must know that all that I possess
            in this round world means less
                to me than this –
        the sweetness of your kiss.

I tell you so with mingled laughter-tears,
    your loving helps to keep at bay my fears.

Picking Blackcurrants

Picking blackcurrants
all one long hot golden afternoon, my fingers
running purple with juice, suddenly
I remembered the amber of your skin
the last time we lay closely together.

I am enchanted
that you want to read me Proust, seeing long
years of contentment stretching ahead;
I top my blackcurrants with new energy
to make them into jam for all those Sunday teas.

Spider

A white linen handkerchief
squared off and folded,
do you still, I wonder, insist
on its use, spurning all offers
of sensible tissues, encased
in a box the blue of your shirt.

Do you still cram your best shirts –
and all else besides –
into crocodile suitcase,
old but much loved, then sit on it hard,
surprised and dismayed when you find
that the lid will no longer shut

* * *

Do you still hide your face, head
buried in pillows,
as you sleep on your front, long arms
bent and flung out like a spider's,
long legs and such elegant feet
dangling from under the duvet.

I can remember so well,
waking to find you
arms and legs wrapped around me, you
making sure I could not escape,
not even to make morning tea,
enmeshed in my loved spider's web.

Book Auction

A tortuous journey:
I was late, I know, and you
must have given up all hope of seeing me.
I let myself into the hall,
stayed at the back
to watch, enthralled,
as your professional face
assessed, dismissed or made a note
of item after item,
weighing your chances,
thin shoulders bent
in total concentration.

A natural break
and I approached
coffee for you in hand;
the light that sprang into your eyes
could well have lit a beacon on the downs
and lit a fire in me.
No time to kiss
but we held hands like children
in that room of children's books.
You led me to the front, asked my advice
and lost the very book you'd come to buy
by turning to explain some point to me.

Last bid, and at a stroke
the hall was emptied.
We briefly kissed – as though this interlude
were part of the order of our days
and not a rare enchantment –
then went opposing ways.
I never told you how I lay all that long night
awake and groaning;

I should have learned from your experience
but only then discovered for myself
how groaning from the heart
could so affect the gut.

Two Love Songs From Greece

1.

If you were here, my bonnie lad,
I'd dance you backwards through the years
and lead you with a steady hand
down endless labyrinthine ways,
so low that we could scarcely stand
and only love marked out our days.

If you were here, my bonnie lad,
I'd stroke your silken silver hair
and taste the sweetness of your breath,
'til all the Grecian nymphs would stare
and cluster at the harbour mouth
to clamour for their rightful share.

If you were here, my bonnie lad,
you'd lie all night within my arms,
I'd bolster up your flagging pride,
sing songs of love as soothing balm,
we'd ride the azure dragonflies
and keep each other safe from harm.

2.

The lips you used to kiss are dry
with waiting for the grass to grow,
the chestnut hair you used to stroke
has lost its once love-burnished glow.
   But, ah my dear, my darling one,
   how glad I am I once was young.

The breasts you cupped in eager hands
are drooping with the weight of years,
the laughter that you loved to hear
is melting in a pool of tears.
   But, ah my dear, my darling one,
   how glad I am I once was young.

The verses that you used to write,
the love songs that you sang to me,
are vanished in a wake of foam
because your boat put out to sea.
 But, ah my dear, my darling one,
 how glad I am I once was young.

Remembering you, as I prepare the Breakfast Grapefruit

Like all good housewives
I have my nightly routine:
dishes to wash and put away,
the breakfast grapefruit to prepare,
cushions to shake and stand upright,
rubbish and the cat – metaphorical –
to put out, doors to lock
and the garden to say Goodnight to.

If you were still here
routine would go by the board,
grapefruit stay cold in the fridge
rubbish be left in the kitchen bin,
the garden and sometimes the doors
left forgotten and unlocked.
There would be no hurry
except the sweet rush to bed.

Then you would teach me again
the hundred and one ways
of loving and being loved;
the cat – still metaphorical –
could sleep on the cushions,
while I slept in your arms
secure in the knowledge
that breakfast would be late.

Dolphin Boy

For six years I kept away from Cornwall
from places I had visited with you,
kept love wrapped up in bandages to hide
the still-sore stump that skin grafts could not heal,
though clever surgeons did their best with it.

Seven is the perfect number, so now
at last I venture nervous foot on ice
thin as an antique mirror over time,
climb Cornish hills that nearly stop the heart
and look for dolphins in the foam-flecked sea.

Where once I watched you swim I sit and dream
gazing far out to sea to find lost hope.
That blaze of blue rolling around the coast
relentless in its tidal stringency,
empty of dolphins loses half its charm.

Always my dolphin boy, you should be here
to lure them to the shore for my delight.

'A Diamond is for Ever'

A yellow diamond –
contradiction in colour –
flamboyant and flash;
a new line in jewellery
thought up by entrepreneurs
greedy for profit.

A diabolical idea:
a synthetic diamond
made from the ashes of the dead
to last for ever,
having no value
except of dubious sentiment.

A love token
only to be worn
on the appropriate finger
when the beloved is dead,
and who shall say
which finger is appropriate?

I loved you in life
and love you still,
but could not wear you as an ornament;
I never flaunted you
and do not wish to flaunt the ashes
of your mortality.

You gave me
butterflies and dragonflies
with jewels in their eyes
gold and silver on their wings,
mementoes of a shared delight –
but never a ring.

I never presumed
to wish for diamonds
other than the words
you flashed upon the page,
nothing about them synthetic –
they'll ring in my head for ever.

Grief is . . .

A bowl brimming over,
waves of emotion
spilling in too-late tears
on the tamped-down soil of memory,
leaving soggy trails
as I trudge wearily to and from the past.

A mist I can't see through,
a shifting barrier of unreason
that nullifies acceptance
of your death, acknowledgement of pain;
map without reference point,
no signposts showing through the gloom.

A time-warp in which
I am enmeshed, present
and past inextricably entangled, so that I
stumble over barriers
newly erected, broken
as I try to push my way clumsily through.

A deep-set guilt, my feelings
my own business and painful
enough in all conscience, as I struggle
to reconcile honesty –
both yours and mine –
with occasional evasion of the truth.

A kind of anger, love crossed
with self-pity and a strange
resentment because you have left me only
a sense of loss, a gap
that no-one else can ever fill,
an emptiness where there should be music.

Whitby Jet

I try to tell past jewelled days as beads
strung on a rosary, their colours shine
but only Whitby jet best suits my needs,
garnet and emerald both listed mine
by right of birth, now more like widow's weeds.

A lifetime's colours fill my mind with pain
they dance in mockery just out of sight –
hard as I try to see them once again
a spreading darkness shuts me out from light
harsh tears spurt faster than wind-driven rain.

The pattern of my days cut clean across
life's multi-coloured layers press me down,
what should have been uplifting turns to dross;
I try to wear my many-jewelled crown
but only Whitby jet befits my loss.

Fanny by Gaslight

The first Christmas without conjecture –
what will it be, your gift to me, and
when will it arrive?
Exotic orchids, freesias
for their colour and their scent –
had I told you they were my mother's
favourite flowers?

Roses, to remind me of the first,
a single red on my unmade bed
left for me to find
after you'd gone; last year's gift
a maple tree,
still small but promising to grow
to all of thirty feet, but not yet
and probably not in my lifetime
nor – now – in yours.

A pill box patterned with violets
lying on dark green velvet, inscribed,
its message *je t'aime.*
'I wondered what you would use it for'
you said, seeing it beside my bed.

Your very first present, a hedgehog,
sharpener for the pencils with which
I scribbled my poems,
More recently a merry-go-round –
I wish you a Merry Christmas
the horses sang
but we never watched them together.

And always, for reading and sharing:
Fanny by Gaslight;
Dance to the Dolphin's Song, the first book
you had ever bought, you said, just for
its title, and, extravagantly,
The Memoirs of Harriette Wilson
for the first sentence.

Your lovely voice reading me to sleep
as I lay in your arms, where I lie
now in memory.

Quiet Day

A quiet rather grey day:
my morning prayer envisaged me
rising to see the light
to hear the wind.
It seemed unlikely
till I heard a voice on the phone speaking
words of comfort from half way up
a bleak mountainside,
the roaring of the wind
waking my spirit to life.

I sit now surrounded by the dead,
a bowl of great golden roses at my feet
another gift of love;
we talk without the need of words
not so much remembering
as being together in that trust
which is the essence
of friendship. I open my arms
to the last to come
and love closes round us.

As arrow prayers reach
to the throne of God,
so my thoughts aspire to the heights of love,
past and present merging into one.
My mind slows,
the wind bloweth where it listeth
images superimpose themselves
as they will,
the how and why cease to matter –
I settle into my quiet day.

Phyllis Louise Wright, 1907- 1999

(Physhe to your Friends)

Even your name
was your own invention;
having used up two in successive careers
you chose one for yourself and your friends.
My mother had Greek leanings, you told me,
covering up the fact that she had nothing to do with it.

Bereft of your childhood by the Great War
spent reading the casualty lists to your mother,
too terrified to look for herself,
you maintained a child's greed for entertainment ever after,
your multi-faceted personality
providing you with at least three successive lives.

You called yourself a Buddhist,
I was never certain if that was a tease
or deep conviction
Certainly you sought the God within yourself
and others, clear-sightedly
and with compassion for our shortcomings.

Disdaining the church, you nevertheless counted
a surprising number of clergy
amongst your friends, called them *holy scroungers,*
plied them with drinks and videos
as you did the rest of us,
listened to their problems
and wisely refrained from too many solutions.

You were a good listener
as well as a good talker, words
were your passion –
spoken, written, recorded, heard and read
you had tried them all
and counted them true,
though you cheated at Scrabble.
Wit salted your conversation,
humour ran in your veins
and saved you from self-glorification.

Not so much an eye for colour
informed your judgement,
as an unfailing instinct for the rightness of things
and for what went with what.
You can't wear those socks with that outfit
you would tell me brusquely,
adding more kindly – *I'll knit you some yellow ones!*

I shall miss the criticism
as much as the kindliness.
You had gone through two lifetimes
before I even met you, still willing
to share all that stored-up knowledge and experience,
full of enthusiasm for what was yet to come.
God gave you a good innings, my friend,
and I think He is not disappointed in your score.

Difficult Concept

A friend's son is dying
of melanoma. Without warning
he has been given six weeks
in which to pack an expectation
of what life might have been,
a last chance to grasp the essence
of its meaning:
>   we must hold on
to the concept of a loving God.

Children everywhere are dying,
in pain, in misery, in fear;
set-faced, rifles at the ready,
they stare out from our
television screens, protagonists
in wars they scarcely understand
but are involved:
>   we must hold on
to the concept of a loving God.

Not all the old are dying;
kept alive by others' care
we get around wearily on sticks
and zimmer-frames. We watch
the young, pray for their chances,
offer them the last lap of our time,
not ours to give:
>   we must hold on
to the concept of a loving God.

The Magi: Kings or Travellers?

Three kings, elected Presidents
their counterparts today, what would they bring:

Gold?
new-minted coinage for the new millennium,
or
receipts for profits made from armaments
sold to the highest bidder either side the war?

Frankincense?
a scented candle, Christmas red and green,
or
stench of burning rubble from a ruined home,
the smell of ashes settling into dust?

Myrrh?
a muslin bag of spices for a Christening cake
or
stronger mixture to embalm the bodies
buried beneath the debris of a bombing raid?

* * *

Three travellers today, wise in the way of prayer
and gentleness, what would they bring?

Gold
of a child's imagining, hope for the future,
faith that the Christmas promises are true?

Frankincense
a floating candle for aromatherapy, and
scent of holiness for meditative prayer?

Myrrh
a perfumed soap to wash away our dirt and
soothing ointment for hurt bodies and hurt minds?

* * *

Which gift would cater for world needs today
and which would the Child accept with joy?

Lost

(for Geoffrey Armstead)

It isn't age I hate,
but cruelty of death-in-life that is dementia,
that first bewilderment before
blankness covers the mind in a sort of comfort,
a thick too-heavy blanket, horse-hair brown
and scratchy, deadening pain but
blotting out awareness of the present
the everyday niceties
that are the 'please' and 'thank you'
of communication.

Such small omissions
spell the onset of a loss of memory,
not not-remembering things
but not knowing even what to do with them:
the crossword clues still almost understood
but answers written in the wrong place,
letters half-formed to look like
hieroglyphics of themselves,
words, jumbled and blown, landing useless
outside conversation.

The sudden terrors
that distort the mind and send one running
from familiarity as fast as from the strange,
loss of a sense of pattern and of place,
no role to fit, routine to follow or philosophy to live by;
a child's delight in naughtiness and mess,
a need for reassurance in a constant flow
by one whose independence brooked
no interference once, a need for love
as well as caring.

As for the carer –
the need to share a pain still unexpressed,
to understand the screaming of frustration,
the urge to strike the kindly hands that help
but don't appreciate attachment to a hairbrush
not one's own, love of a gaudy dressing gown,
rejection of the tawdry cracker gift,
snatches of songs and hymns rendered
at awkward moments, and rare gestures of affection
that can break the heart.

Rest Home

Lottie slaps my face,
she says I got her chair.
As if I care
where I sit
in this airless space that wraps me round –
nothing of comfort to be found,
it's not my place.

They think I can't remember who I am
or where I used to be –
as if I give a damn
who's here or not here
when I am not there,
there where I ought to be,
my own things round me
and the smell of roses
that I grew for pot-pourri –
they say that is my bedroom over there.

These horrid rows of chairs
make nonsense of this place they call a home,
they drag us to the toilet every hour,
lock the front door in case we wander far.
We sit like children in a bleak schoolroom
but there's no school, no teacher and no class,
no playground chatter
with the day's best friend.

No fun in this place,
only Christmas brings a hint of cheer,
deep voices sing under the windows,
Christmas carols ring
loud on the frosty air –
no Jack Frost patterns
on the glass inside
and words we used to know so well are lost.

Call this a party! –
Where's my mother then?
She should be here
or it's no sort of show,
no-one to call me clarty when I slop
trifle on my new dress,
help me mop up the mess
and wipe my fingers on her handkerchief
smelling of Devon violets.

Here comes a juggler
tossing balls of string
high up towards the ceiling –
there's a thing
good string should not be wasted in this rationing,
oh, now he's playing with a pack of cards!
They drag us back, back to the rows of chairs
and bring out the balloons –
I've always hated them.

Bring on the dancers,
I can sit and watch,
could never do the steps,
made a right botch
if I tried waltzing or fox-trot;
I couldn't follow through,
could never let myself be led or shown
and no boy ever picked me on the spot.
But now a stranger pulls me to my feet –
he's got a lovely smile –
he puts his hands on mine
and lets me lead him
where I want to go.

Clouds of Glory in Reverse

Would it have been better, Lord,
if we'd been born mature and wise,
ears fully open to the word,
knowing duplicity and lies
for what they are, seeing the worst
in human-kind as well as best,
accepting evil from the first
not putting each good to the test.

And would it not have made more sense
if we'd grown young with time instead
of old, ripened to innocence,
not lingered here till we are dead
dead to all reason, incapable
of listening to heart or head
or knowing we are culpable.

Seeing in childhood with old eyes,
we'd bring experience to bear
on all the pettiness and lies
that adults use when they declare
a child should learn to hold its tongue,
and, understanding all too well
the ills of age, of wear and tear,
of effort needed not to sell
ourselves too soon to others' care,
we'd have no fear of dying young.

Satan, God, and the Apple

(for Michael Starr)

When Eve first tempted Adam
with the apple of desire,
the serpent smiled to know his
trick had worked, its firm ripe flesh
tart on the tongue, and flavour
in the mouth all bitter-sweet.

Cut through from stem to stern
an apple bears the mark of sin,
the devil's thumb-print plainly seen:
erotic image deep within its heart,
its sweetness smirched, despoiled
by the blackened pips of lust.

God's plans are not so easily
destroyed, nor is his scheme
for human-kind to be confounded
by man's greed or Satan's wiles;
cut now across the grain, an apple
shows a new design – a star.

To break a fast with apples is
small sin, acidity fit penance,
the star within symbol of hope
redemption and the birth of Christ,
God smiles to see his work revealed,
'Foiled again, poor devil!' he declares.

Baptism

(for Francesca Hickey)

Such a long journey, so many twists
and turns along the way; you must
carry your candle carefully, to light
the dark corners, shine through the
clouds that sometimes fill the sky.

Such a long journey, but always
you will have water for your needs,
streams running clear above chalk,
cold and refreshing when the way is
hard, with the sun hot on your back.

Such a long journey, but you travel
by faith, ours as well as your own;
you need have no fear for the cross
on your brow or the courage it takes
to explain that you know it is there.

Such a long journey, but each step
you take will be watched by us all
cheering you on as you go; be happy,
Francesca, and dance down the years,
we wish you Godspeed as you pass.

The Finger Of God

Walking through the arch
on past the abbey's squared-off solidity,
the patch of new-cut grass
beneath the finger of God,
I struggle to keep up
with my father's expectant stride
into what is for him a new experience.

He pauses to look up
at stained glass windows from the outside,
seeing his own Cathedral in his mind's eye –
he does not need to tell me this,
nor that he reverently touches
the bark of a tree
growing on the bank beside
a wider river and a larger bridge.

He flicks a litter of paper aside
with the point of his stick
and leans on the bridge we have reached,
observes the paddling with a curious eye,
touches my arm for support, and waits
for what it is I have brought him to see.

His eyes scan the river
and I see a younger man,
weighed down with a half-plate camera
stalking the swans on Bassenthwaite,
and, earlier still,
getting out of bed
not quite better of pneumonia
to walk across the frozen Wear.

Now his heart leaps with the salmon
and I, too, exult
because I have brought him in old age
to a small new happiness.

Durham Allotments

*'Professors going to dig their tea
are overlooked in their library of earth
by the Cathedral towers. To me
the whole May scene is held for ever
in a special sort of Saturday afternoon weather.'*
David Scott

My father's allotment was on Mount Joy,
the last place where the monks rested when
they carried St Cuthbert's body, and before
they met the old woman with her dun cow
and christened their place Dunholme.

He was a Bede man and had loved the city
from his youth, in age he rested on its piety,
antiquity and peace. He grew the flowers he loved,
roses for my mother, amid all manner of exotica –
vegetables whose names we scarcely knew.

He grew yellow tomatoes, the first I'd ever seen,
sold Christmas trees for church funds and
replanted them each year when people
needed to get rid of them. Younger men
did his heavy digging and he their watering.

We lived in Mount Joy Crescent, sheltered
by the holy hill and with a view of the Cathedral
from the bathroom window – we took our visitors
to admire it and the hardier among them climbed
to my attic to see it through the skylight.

We were happy there, scoffed at our friends
who worried that we lived in number 13,
refused to believe that superstition could have
caused my mother's death when she fell
down the cellar stairs and our lives fell apart.

Those allotments live on in my heart, though
they were obliterated years ago and the new
science block stands where they once were;
a special sort of summer weather is always there
and I am happy that professors still dig.

Head High

(A Poem about my father, for U.A.Fanthorpe)

The youngest of eleven children, a sickly child,
my father's weakness proved to be his strength;
destined to follow his brothers down the pit, he
flouted tradition, went his chosen way, left school
to go back as a pupil teacher the next week.

Unsuspecting, he opened the door one morning –
an early bluestocking, fresh from the local Tech,
responded to his smile, and he was hooked,
hers for life; he followed her to college, where
they lived on twin hills at St Hild and St Bede.

What his parents made of it is not on record, though
her father disapproved; an invalid, he watched the
young man waiting, swinging on the garden gate
and muttered 'that must be stopped' but there
was no stopping my father when his heart was set.

'Here comes old Bewick, apologising for existing
as usual' a college friend once said of him, but
a steady determination lurked behind the shyness,
the self-effacement which was his stock-in-trade;
he knew that some things were worth waiting for.

1914: C3, he got himself into the army and over
to France, only to be sent straight back again;
later he boasted that his Christmas dinner on the
voyage home was three sucks of a thermometer.
Demobbed, he got a headship and fathered me.

He gave me the freedom of the world of books,
talked of his favourite Dickens characters as live,
quoted Browning and Tennyson, recited rhyme.
His son had died in infancy and never by word or
look did he make me think I should have been a boy.

His own first book was a complete Shakespeare
for which he walked eight miles there and back
asking the bookseller to keep it for him. He, knowing
truth when he saw it, said 'take it and pay me weekly'
a tale my father could never recount without a tear.

Nothing was too strenuous for a girl to attempt or to
attain; he took me walking, showed me how to place
my feet on downward slopes, how not to fear a fall.
'However difficult the way has been or how tiring,
he said 'always walk the last mile with your head up.'

Young Woman on a Swing

(for John Greening)

I found it with his treasures when he died:
a sepia photograph, its edges curled,
young woman on a swing, grave, steady-eyed.

All his own work, why did he need to hide
her likeness from the still incurious world?
I found it with his treasures when he died.

A classic pose, head proud and turned aside
as if she read the future there unfurled,
young woman on a swing, grave, steady-eyed.

I doubt she let him take her for a ride,
real or imagined, as her long skirt swirled;
I found her with his treasures when he died.

Until the day when she became his bride
he was too shy to dance, nor ever whirled
his woman on a swing, grave, steady-eyed.

She never crossed him and she never lied,
he was her life, the focus of her world;
I found her with his treasures when he died:
my mother on a swing, grave, steady-eyed.

The Face in the Mirror

I followed her around –
as always on my first night home –
talking and listening,
catching up on news and gossip,
on just being together,
slowly unravelling the threads
of intimacy stored like cotton reels
in the weeks we had been apart.

I followed her
into her bedroom,
watched while she curled her hair,
her face a perfect oval
reflected in the mirror.
Then we both laughed
and hugged each other hard,
so that I saw her face
reflected over mine
before we went our separate ways to bed.

Next day she died – quite suddenly –
I wasn't even there to see her go,
to hold her hand or hug her one last time.
We cleared the house
and brought my father south,
tempering strangeness with a few familiar pieces,
her bedroom suite for me –
at last a full-length mirror of my own.

Forty years later I still use the glass
to test a hem-line,
tidy up my hair,
or just to look behind myself
hoping to find
the perfect oval of my mother's face.
I favour father's side
but sometimes now I see
heart-stopping glimpses of her likeness
reflected there in me.

December Primrose

(for Stella Davis)

Neither nothing nor something,
a drear December day
hanging untidily between
Christmas and a New Year
for which I have no energy.

Tomorrow is the anniversary
of my parents' wedding,
which I must summon up
the strength to celebrate –
surely the beginning of me.

I always sent my mother the first
snowdrops – a birthday package –
carefully wrapped in tissue, early
primroses and a small jar of Devon
Violets tucked inside the wrapping.

Separate and special, two or three
from my garden in a good year;
this year, braving the frost, one
small hardy primrose shows
bright yellow against the grey.

I'll pick it tomorrow and think
of her, struggling so hard
to understand a teenager
who rebelled at every step, and
fights for independence still.

The Durham Coast

(for Don Barnard)

A photograph of Horden beach: the sea
far out, a stretch of strangely dark brown sand,
then stones too large for pebbles, sea-washed
and splendid, deep blue and cinnamon,
streaked and patterned till they merge into
a great curve of colour, shouting to the sky.
I remember those stones so well, the feel of
them, the rough the smooth, the pockmarked
and the shell-shaped – those you could hold
to your ear to hear the sound of the sea,

But the Durham coast was different then,
wearing its layer of coal-dust as a woman might
a shawl, old and weathered, rough, and grey.
We paddled in a smutty sea, built our castles
with black sand and, if we lingered late,
saw the men riding their bicycles home,
sacks of sea-coal slung awkwardly across.
Their faces were black masks, oddly clownlike
strange holes for sunken eyes, mouths that
hollered greetings in untranslatable pitmatic.

* * *

Mother and the Aunts came with us most days
to the beach, paddling with skirts tucked into
their voluminous bloomers, hands holding our
reluctant hands, carrying bucket and spade.
I never went far into the sea, preferring to play
in the rock pools, collecting small pebbles or
knobbly pieces of seaweed, leaving the crabs;
I loved the beach shop, higher up the cliff
where we bought black bullets and sherbert dabs,
fingering balloons and rows of tricycles and toys.

The shop has disappeared, walkway and cliff
worn away to nothing by the impersonal cruelty
of time and the crumbling nature of rock.
The harbour with its swimming pool, where
my sister was thrown in on the end of a rope
to teach her to swim – or drown – is larger
and cleaner, and the rails where the bogeys
ran down with their cargo of coal to the ships
are no longer there. Progress has effaced
its landmarks, but I still read my history here.

9 Across

Little balls of soap and water:
a crossword clue to take the magic
out of bubbles, ethereal amethysts,
blown through the tunnel of memory
from the clay pipe of my childhood.

I thought diamonds should have been
the colour of amethysts, the fuss
everyone made of them, and I loved
my grandmother's amethyst ring
that I inherited along with her name
and lost to a sneak-thief at work.

My sister chose a witch-ball for
her eighteenth birthday, a sparkling
glass bubble, its surface like shot silk;
delivered by the shop, it arrived
in fragments to shatter her illusions.

Magic never lasts, we learn that as we
grow older, but the force of our gaze
can fix its bubbles for a time; suspended
in air they hang in the mind and when
they break we pick up the fragments
and frame them as stained glass.

Geoffrey Armstead

Mentor, Priest and Friend:
On the occasion of your retirement
from St. Bartholomew's, Hyde.

When still a schoolboy you declared yourself
prepared to be God's fool, yet, foreordained
to be his instrument, you could not know
that over forty years would pass before
you could accept your own beneficence.

Uncertain still, on looking back on life –
itself an exercise you deprecate –
you single out the errors and wrong turns
with which to castigate yourself, the lack
of confidence which leaves you vulnerable.

Honest enough to look within yourself
facing your doubts with courage to survive,
you carried many of us part-way home,
not caring if it took you off the road
you'd meant to tread when setting out alone.

We stand now in your strength, our own renewed,
and those who died along the way did so
in better heart for your unfailing care;
my prayer for you is that, accepting need,
you let yourself be carried in your turn.

Five Pips a Week

I read somewhere recently that an orange
– or was it a grapefruit? – is said to be seedless
when it has less than five pips.
So everything is relative, my back hurts
only when I think about it, and an honest person
is one who never tells a lie more that four times
a week, month, year or whatever.

Call me peculiar, old-fashioned, pedantic
north country, outspoken or blunt,
but to me an orange is seedless only
when it has no pips, my back hurts
all the time, and an honest person
is one who always tells the truth
no matter what the cost.

Displaced

I yearn for little shops,
for sugar in blue bags,
bacon cut thick or thin
with cleanly slicing blades,
potatoes dripping soil
proud in my father's hands,
washed ready for the pan,
eaten within the hour.

This is not my world:
this place of push and shove,
of supermarket queues,
the tight-packed shelves
presenting foreign face
to be explored, stiff rows
of prepacked ready meals
to rush home and refreeze.

This is not my pace,
a race to defile the moon
with brash impetuosity
and instant new technology;
each television programme
a virtual reality; e-mail
by easicom – *love equals 20,*
attachments are removed.

Trying out this and that
testing a few new skills,
making discoveries,
drawing fresh conclusions,
but earthed in my own time
at my own speed of change;
too old to rush, I tag along
behind the century.

Where the Lovebirds Sang

(for Clem and Graham Bannell)

Here the lovebirds sang,
quick blue against white tile
dug from the earth, and in the corner
a greengage tree provided shade;
though ready now for picking
its fruit goes unremarked.

Sunflowers, high,
fronting the warm brick wall
look down on lesser flowers
and on the Druids' circle,
a lush and vivid green
mysteriously soft and giving.

The surface of the pond
is proud with water-lilies,
loud with a colony of frogs;
against the fence, billets
of stout wood surround
hearthstones garnered from the soil.

Fat pink foxgloves,
smile on a blue-green sea of heartsease,
forget-me-nots,
and sweet peas; agapanthus,
like tall bluebells, smells
of the tobacco plant close by.

Eyes bright with dreams, a boy
fingers his new backgammon board,
its jewelled counters gleaming
in the sun; down the years I see,
at that same garden bench, old men
who play on as the shadows fall.

'Sweet and Harsh, Harsh and Sweet'

(for Lorraine Curtis)

I stand by his stone in the graveyard
where the air is harsh and sweet,
the wind blows off the Atlantic
to the sound of dancing feet,
and the words of the greatest poet
in Ireland's pattern of rhyme
ring round on the hills like chanting
to last till the end of time.

The clouds lie low on Ben Bulben
where their shadows race and play,
and the hurt of a hundred years lives on
in the setting of today;
my heart is full of his sorrow,
my head is heavy with pain,
his words wring the core of pity dry
that waits for the gentle rain.

Gorse blazes from the hedgerows
as the low stone walls run down
to the brooding sea beneath them
and on into Sligo town;
my candle burns by the limestone cross,
winds lift it heaven-high,
sun lights the distant pathway
and the horseman passes by.

Chagall Window at Chichester

Red as his heart's wild blood, Chagall
splashed onto glass the meaning of
his art, painting the light behind
the colours that he used, against
an abstract glow small bright figures
praising God in the firmament.

Triumphal purple and deep blue –
colours of Heaven on earth –
patches of strong yellow he loved,
touches of white beside fierce red;
the poet quiet in green cloak
with donkey head and open book,
setting the music to his words.

Musicians leap to the foreground:
cymbals and drum, trumpet and horn
resounding in rivalry, each
of them crying 'Listen to me!'
The psalmist, mounted on an ass,
serenely plays his harp, and smiles.

The people are in festive mood:
under the window is a jazz
extravaganza – echoes of
Ellington – golden trumpets sound
in homage to the Duke and to
the Lord. The poet winks and adds
his scribblings to the paean of praise.

Mother Goose's Daughter

A fortunate lifetime of feathers:
sleeping on a feather bed as a child,
shaking its Mother Goose softness;
snug under a duvet since the first Puffin
imported from Norway, smoothing
its feathered shape each morning.

A high feather bed at my Granny's
on a Victorian bedstead that creaked,
with round brass knobs at each corner
that I twiddled till they fell off, waiting
in the excited dawn for Christmas to begin,
to suck the orange from my stocking toe.

A bed-chair at home when visitors stayed:
too little space for a plump child, the arms
hard and constraining as I tried to turn;
brown velvet cushions for a mattress, a long
feather bolster on top for comfort, the fire
flickering before it went out where I slept.

My first trip abroad at seventeen, feathers
in my pen friend's painted wooden bed;
watching her dress in dirndl and white blouse.
Mutti, sie kann sprechen, she exclaimed
that first morning, when weariness
and shyness fell away to loosen my tongue,

Greek beds over the years, each one
harder than the last; a thin blanket spread
over the mattress makes little difference
so I take my own feather duvet to lie on;
the turning wheel slows to a halt, I shake
my childhood's feathers out over the sea.

Traditional Recipe

In the old year's last hour
of daylight, I baked a cake,
a traditional Dundee
according to the recipe,
though my cakes are rarely
wholly traditional –
there is always something
not in the cupboard
that has to be left out,
and something additional
that has to be included
just for the hell of it.

My Christmas cake
sits in the tin un-iced,
to be eaten later with cheese,
a piece to be saved tonight
for the first-foot who will not come.
The old traditions crowd
my mind, the loved dead
walk in slow procession,
lingering to bless and
to be recognised again
as the progenitors
of all that I hold dear.

My mother was baking
for us when she died
though that was March –
Good Friday, another dark day.
The inevitable *if only* she
had not gone to the cellar
to put something away;
my greatest regret:
that I never had a daughter
to whom I could pass on
the love she gave me
and the skills she taught.

Oranges at Christmas Time

I can see our dining-room still:
the sideboard with its central mirror,
heavy two-handled fruit bowl
doubled by its own reflection
in the glass; round red Jonathans
polished to perfection, Jaffa oranges
and sometimes pears; no rules
forbidding us to touch – they were there
for the picking.

At Christmas there were tangerines
for eating at the table after meals.
A conniving uncle taught us how to spit
the pips backwards into the fire
without getting up from our chairs,
my mother indulgent to his goings-on.
He was the same uncle who tickled us
till we screamed for mercy then drew
breath to ask for more.

Last Christmas I was given a tree,
a Citris Mitis, fragrant with flowers
growing in clusters, perfectly formed,
delicate and white, five small oranges
appearing at the same time. They
ripened to perfection and I used
them in my next batch of marmalade,
alongside the Sevilles and the limes,
and it tasted fine.

New oranges upon my tree this year,
rich colour set to music and to rhyme,
their succulence a secret learned
in childhood, schooled by my mother's
tolerance – acceptance of the aunt who
taught us to suck oranges messily
through a sugar lump, thrust deep into
a hole made through the rind, to reach
the flesh beneath.

Oranges at Christmas time, memory
sharp as their flavour, sweet as the
indulgences of childhood and the lasting
power of love.

Chip off the old Block

(for Rob Evans)

Born in a northern city,
nurtured on dripping
and the finest lard,
I made my earliest outings
wrapped in thin pages
of the Sports Gazette,
printed on baby pink.

Bottle-brown vinegar.
salt from a squat blue can,
sprinkled my adolescence
and aroused my fire,
a need for something more –
tomato sauce, H.P. or worse –
stunted my growth.

In age my energy subsides,
and hopes of taste
with this new fatness fade;
divested of the plastic wrap
from supermarket shelves,
I'm labelled oven-ready
and dished up on a plate.

Not another Poem about Deafness!

If I'd been born deaf
would it have been easier to bear,
better to have spent my time
learning sign language,
reading people's lips and their minds,
rather than using loops that don't work
and hearing aids that squeak?

Would people have been kinder,
gentler, more considerate,
have pulled me to the front,
made certain that I understood
what was going on,
not produced a mad jumble of sound
by all talking at once?

Would it have hurt even more
being shut out,
cut off from the group,
pushed back from the centre of things;
would I have been just as distressed
at not being able to hear
what other people need.

It's not just missed conversation,
sharing of thoughts and ideas,
quick humour and wit,
cut and thrust
and quick repartee –
the inconsequential remarks
still need to be properly heard.

The worst is being ignored
when they say *never mind,*
it wasn't important,
you didn't miss much –
but what did I miss?
I wasn't talking to you
is the ultimate snub.

Then there are people who whisper
or mumble, turn their heads to one side
or cover their mouths with their hands;
they just can't be bothered
to look at your face,
their heads on their chests
when they make a remark.

My friend Jenny and I
laugh together a lot – or cry –
at their want of real thought.
Where's Jenny now?
I called her downstairs
as I came in the door –
I forgot she can't hear me!

Dues Paid?

(for Mieke Hooker)

Tidied my life,
paid all my dues,
naught left to do but pack
and say 'Goodbye'.

Paid all my dues?
Wrung the last drop
from every passing day,
savoured the juice,
said grace before and after?

Accepted night?
Grateful for sleep that came,
using bought time for thought
when sleep denied, conserving energy,
gritting my teeth against the pain?

Remembered childhood?
Told love and thanks to family
and that great multitude
of relatives, always around,
greedy with need
to be appreciated?

Told all my friends
how much they mean to me?
Received their kindness gratefully,
held out a hand
to those who needed it
much as I do myself?

Appreciated things, music
and colour, painting and poetry,
revelled in words,
loved rhyme and given thanks
for that small talent,
God's own gift to me?

Paid all my dues?
Dear God, I need more time
to parcel out my thanks
and pour my love
on all I value here;
not just a breathing space,
time to draw breath
and sing your praise.

Hallucinations

(for Mr W.H. Fowler)

The first stumble into an alien world,
blackness and a frightening dizziness,
clutching a passing stranger,
sitting on a bench at Hyde Gate
beside the acacia tree,
Spring bursting from its lime-green foliage,
a nightmare darkness growing in my head.

Feet like the elephant's child
after a few hours of heat,
plodding tiredly around the town;
waking to the high-fashion world
of hospital nighties, sweetly sprigged,
backless pattern, modesty nil,
feet now semi-paralysed and swollen.

Arriving in a colourful world,
myself an Oriental princess
swathed in purple and orange,
groomed and pampered, bathed and perfumed,
plied with rich food, sauces and fine wines,
waited on by fawning courtiers,
chemists moving in the perfumery below.

A hush, unholy and macabre, pervaded all
until I sensed their perfume was not to be distilled
for me but of me, to enhance their future race.
Never was vision so swiftly torn apart
as I hot-dreamt back to feverish normality, though
not so normal as to trust my friends, accusing them
of poisoning me when they proffered ice cream
on a spoon or tea to suck through a straw.

Moving to a world of travel: a trip
to New York with strangers, meeting
an old friend to be taken to the sights:
Times Square, Greenwich Village, Macey's
and all the best restaurants, one in particular
with wonderful cuisine and exotic decor,
walls covered in velvet, and ceilings
with great squares of soft cream satin.

Suddenly a gang, armed to the teeth
erupted into the room. We shinned up the walls
and clung, terrified, to the satin squares of ceiling,
clawing our way through by the skin of our heels
and out into the hospital car-park
unaccountably full of caravans.
I wake to the squares of ceiling in the ward,
they loom over me with new menace.

Institutionalised, cossetted, wrapped
in the discipline of hospital red tape,
bullied onto sticks to tap the corridors
and practise walking up and down the stairs,
I settle into a comforting routine,
shaken suddenly by rush and confusion.
*We need you out, we need your space
for mud-caked soldiers back from France.*

Waking I find myself indeed expelled,
my bed now needed for another's miracle;
will I survive, will courage be enough to bear
my weight along, keep damaged spine upright?
Wheeled past the windows, seeing there
a second acacia tree, same vivid shade of green,
the scent of summer beckoning beyond
the open door, I set out on a new adventure.

Singleton

(for the Staff of Singleton Ward, The Mount, Bishopstoke.)

Good Night, My Darling, I love you,
Good Night, My Darling, Good Night.

It is 5 a.m.: a watery dawn trickles thinly
through ward windows
to outline six figures sleeping peacefully
and one who cannot sleep.

They stir uneasily as I sit up to read,
pull curtains around my cubicle
and fumble for the postcard
which should mark my page.

Green trousers, blue trousers, striped
overalls and sensible or platform shoes;
watchful of need, trim figures pace the floor,
leave us to sleep again as best we can.

I settle back, accept a draught
against the pain, wriggle my bottom
to relieve sciatic nerves and
lose myself in blessed print again.

Good Night, My Darling,
Good Night, My Darling,
I love you – Good Night.

Day breaks at last, chairs shift,
commodes are wheeled away,
bodies are bathed, hair washed,
rollers inserted and removed.

Ladies, transformed, smile
thankfully, sink back to sleep
until their visitors arrive,
rouse only for a cup of tea.

The men's side is more curious,
propel themselves into the day room,
watch cricket or the News,
cast tolerant eyes on me with 'Weakest Link'.

My blind friend watches shapes
but cannot see the ball.
Our Dutchman tells us vigorously
how proud he is that he is Dutch.

A tail emaciated figure leans against
the window bars, whimpers with nerves
and looks just like my Richard might have done
if he'd achieved old age and yet more pain.

And Jim, our Petty Officer, torpedoed twice,
supported by his faithful wife,
keeps up his monologue by day and night.

Good Night, My Darling, Good Night,
I love you, My Darling Good Night.

Confusion

(for Joyce Crawford)

I know what it feels like:
lying flat with nothing to look at
but the metal pipes
that criss-cross the ceiling in bizarre patterns
of rigidity.

Later they come into use
for drawing the curtains round the beds,
enclosing each of us
in what is meant to be a cocoon of privacy
but is a prison.

Confused and tearful
the new patient lies, convinced it is late
and she has not eaten,
not remembering the visitors who came
with flowers and love.

Three weeks is not long
to get used to the fear of total dependency,
but long enough
to recognise the stark terror of skidding
out of control.

I lend her my teddy
for something to cuddle, his brown velvet coat
a comfort in the dark;
I lie wakeful myself, her pain and confusion
reflecting my fear.

Ice Hockey at the Day Hospital

(for Dr. J. Duffy)

Special Delivery:
collected each Monday morning –
too early for my liking –
welcomed with kind words,
comforting cups of tea,
coffee, and rich tea biscuits.

Expected to relax
and chat to our neighbour –
mine is usually asleep so I make
an effort to talk to someone else,
exchange symptoms and small talk
across the intervening table.

Slowly the circle
fills; I am carried off to have
a memory test: name, date of birth,
today's date, count backwards
from twenty to nought. *Nothing wrong
with your memory*, sister says.

Little does she know
how I search for words sometimes,
struggle with the shape of what
is in my head, can't give it a name.
But for now I am accepted,
returned to the circle; exercises next.

Simple stretching that
is surprisingly difficult, parallel bars,
obstacles to step over, balls to bounce,
hoops to throw, wobbly rubber mats
to balance on and a fair imitation
of Winchester High Street to negotiate.
Netball for a change
soft balls to throw into a low net;
a fierce game of ice-hockey

two opposing teams with plastic sticks
and pucks. I score a goal –
my first ever – and am roundly cheered.

Variously exhausted
we gather in threesomes for lunch:
I talk to a quiet man who suddenly says
he retired early to have time with his wife,
he still misses her; I manage a smile
and a few words that I hope he hears.

Hospital Plumbing

These good-looking young men
lean and clean, confident in shirt sleeves,
how can they pronounce
on our bowels and brains, as if
the hospital plumbing
needed attention, our bodies
a sub-section of the same system,
working to the turn of a screw
or the adjustment of a piece of chain
clanking into place?

They want to make us fit
so that the last piece of the pattern
can slide into place and their diagrams
look tidy again.

Victoria Ward, R.H.C.H, 12.10.05

Tristesse

A sunny room, more sky between the trees
than seen from my loved collage near the park,
where council parsimony keeps me dark
and only winter offers space to breathe.
Here Autumn colours dizzying the breeze
make moving patterns on far lines of chalk,
some branches showing sections of pared bark –
I fear I see them stripped before I leave.

Six of us captive here, just thoughts for food
to last us through the slowly turning hours,
as we rekindle hearts and minds to yearn
for life as it was lived and reckoned good:
we mourn lost dignity and failing powers,
the walls seep sorrow for the heartbreak seen.

Clifton Ward (Medical Elderly), R.H.C.H.
October, 2005.

Guy Fawkes in D Ward

(for Sylvia Lofstedt, the only one of us who stayed awake.)

Six ill-assorted women take their ease
in various postures, stretched out on a bed,
sprawled on a chair, semi-supported by
straw pillows at strange angles at its head.

Past eight o'clock and darkness holds the ward;
lucky to have a window on the night
we hold our breath like children round the fire
of Guy Fawkes' shame and centuries' delight.

Next morning, sharing colours of our dreams
we find that only one of us could hold
bright patterns on the edges of the dark,
the rest made do with bonfires long grown cold.

I still remember in our small back yard
my father lighting fireworks for the street,
the spit of Catherine wheel and rocket hiss
while cracker in his pocket burnt his seat.

Clifton Ward (Medical Elderly) R.H.C.H.
6th November, 2005.

Christmas in D Ward

Christmas, they tell us, maybe
a chance of getting home.
What's home to us now? –
a bed on one side or the other
it's all the same, a place that's
daily cleaned as we are. A solemn
Polish orderly sweeps out the dust
without a word.

But every now and then he hurls
himself at the window, standing
on the sill, his hands flat on
the glass, an expression
of despair on his face as he
gazes into the night sky.
He has a wife and child
out there somewhere.

The new maternity wing lies
just outside, for him sightworthy
or sight unseen? I lie
wakeful, worry infecting heart
and mind. What can I do
about it anyway, I have no
hostages to fortune, or
promises to break.

I take the evening paper left
by a bored visitor, look at the page
of winter coats, now
only three hundred pounds.
Opposite is an appeal for aid, how
thirty pounds can save a baby's life –
I cringe under my cotton blanket,
know what I must do.

A Driftwood Cross

(for Kay Cotton, who made it.)

A piece of driftwood carved into a cross,
the marks of nails and spear already gouged
and depth of colour running red as blood.

Initial skilful cutting with a knife,
long hours of sanding, patience, love and pain
all these embodied, wrought into the wood;

promise of resurrection clearly seen,
cut in the surface flowers of love and hope
that grow with contemplation of the rood.

I hold it in my hand and draw such strength
from feeling the close texture of the grain,
the hardness and the faithfulness of wood.

Strong tides are running still within its heart,
the timelessness and turbulence of sea
reflecting human nature's every mood;

my own dark moods of bitterness and doubt,
not knowing if I'd ever walk again,
held deep within the promise of the wood.

No Space on their forms for Hate

They came to assess my needs,
talked happily of walking, no car
on that golden October morning.

Could they not see my needs
clear on my face as hatred in
my heart, did they need to ask?

They wrote it all down, details of
dependence, my need for help –
no space on their forms for hate.

Hate is a fuel fierce as anger,
a spur to contrivance and action,
expressing my will to survive.

* * *

It has its place, this catalogue of need
they urge, extract from me like teeth,
force me to recognise, put into words.

Oh yes, I'll walk again, but not the hills
that gave me such delight, I'll pace
low paths with something like content.

Stronger than hate, love will suffice
to get my clockwork on the move,
love that needs love to help it on its way.

Without the love of friends I'd not survive
and doubt I'd even want to, but
acknowledging dependence still breeds hate.

Colours glow strongly when they are still wet

Colours glow strongly when they are still wet
their luminescence adding depth to tone,
the sea's an angry azure in a fret

but, come to think of it, it's never let
to harden on a canvas or a stone,
colours glow strongly when they are still wet.

My purple ink's the best I'll ever get
for writing bawdy poems near the bone;
the sea's an angry azure in a fret

and green glass balls secure a fishing net
left floating on its gleaming depths alone –
colours glow strongly when they are still wet.

Rich jewels gain new lustre when they're set,
the sheen of gold enhancing colour tone;
the sea's an angry azure in a fret,

its white-topped riders rising higher yet
till storm winds blow the waves to crash and moan,
colours glow strongly when they are still wet,
the sea's an angry azure in a fret.

Things Half-remembered

(for Lorraine Curtis)

The things just half-remembered are to blame,
they stimulate lost thought and tease the mind
to find the jig-saw pieces left behind.

The book once read, no author and no name,
only an essence or a sense of place
to help to fill once-treasured reading space.

A painting hanging on a wall somewhere,
a group of figures carved from ageing trees
long since worn down by weather: rain and breeze.

Music, half-heard, still hanging on the air
subtle as perfume, never quite recalled,
no recollection save of being enthralled.

A picture village glimpsed when driving past
now out of context clueless, and no way
to reconstruct a perfect summer day.

A corner of old London, built to last
but fleeting as an image, full of grace
though never found again for dwelling-place.

People not seen for years, impressions fade:
at ten a boy I met on holiday,
twenty, a Welshman fancied for a day.

More recently a score of colleagues laid
in tissued layers, figures on a list
obscured by others in a shifting mist.

Seventy-Seven to Seven

(for Tayla on her seventh birthday)

Seven is the perfect number
for all sorts of reasons:
seven days in the week,
seven wonders of the world
and seven seas around it
everlastingly uncurled.

What they tell you isn't true,
it isn't even fair –
it isn't any harder being grown
than being half-way there;
keep your eyes fixed on the stars
and you'll never fall too far.

I know because I'm there –
ten times your age, and seven
times all your fingers
plus another seven more,
as many as you have of years
and still no time for tears.

So I play my games with words
and twist them seven times,
then turn them into rhymes
to write a poem for you,
and you could do this too –
why, you already do!

Shadow Games

(for Kaysha Baker, aged 8)

I glance up from the sink where I'm getting a drink
and a shadow goes over one eye. I look all around
me from ceiling to floor, not a thing to be found
nor a knock on the door, but I know, a stranger
walked through the kitchen and no-one was there but I.

I go on upstairs, past the bathroom door
that someone has left pulled close to. I shiver
and shake at the thought of who's there, though
I know that it's nobody new, just the old goblin
who's lived there for years under the flush in the loo.

I settle in bed, pull the clothes on my head
and hope I will sleep the night through, but my
wallpaper's patterned in stripes and strange marks
that turn into tigers and worse in the dark,
they keep me awake with the noise that they make.

They crawl in beside me, take over my dreams
and fight me with knives, forks and spoons.
If I had the courage, I'd leave them right there,
jump out through the window and on the moon's chair
hitch a lift to the back of a cloud, where I'd stay till next day
when they all went away, and I'd think of a new game to play.

Seascape, Portland

I step inside; the sea
held in my heart
these past months, rises
to my ears, rivets my gaze.
All day I watch it,
hear it all night long:
that drum-roll rhythmic
pounding of the waves,
a rattling hiss of pebbles
dragged back from the shore.

There is such music
in my head, its melody
the rhythm of the sea,
new tunes in-rolling
with the tide. New words
would take more time;
charting the changes
demands a fresh approach
with each incoming wave,
each view encapsulated.

Afterglow of sunset
is a new experience
mysterious as a mirage,
tangible as place,
minarets and mountains
of a child's imagination
seen in the sky. The moon
at full creates a pathway
all the way to France
across the shining sea.

        * * *

Remembered vastness
of the sea and sky

widens enclosing view
of church and churchyard –
King Alfred's grave
flat un-named stone,
plain cross the only mark –
by this I choose to live,
but in my ears
the sea is sounding still.

Fortuneswell

A huddle of grey-white stone
below the undercliff
shapes these drunken terraces,
hanging precariously at the sea's edge.

A broken jigsaw of small shops
runs up the steep slope,
pieces interlocking
in a pattern of nonconformity.

Narrow openings between the houses
rush precipitously down to the sea
walls almost touching in their haste,
gulls karking loudly overhead.

Standing at the halfway point
on a balcony slightly askew,
encompassing the stretch of sea
from Alleluia Bay to Chesil Beach,

I look into the setting sun,
where a long ladder leads
behind the clouds, their crimson
fading to incongruous salmon pink.

Trailing assorted ribbons
it sinks heavily below the sea,
and an impenetrable forest
spreads to the edge of the sky.

The little terraces close up against
the dark, their faces are reborn
when street lamps one by one appear
and spread their blessing on the night.

Fortuneswell, II

Light rushes to meet me
as I walk up the stairs,
the sea shouts 'Look at me,
look at me now!'
The surge and the swell,
that I come back to see
welcome me in,
rock me in rhythm,
fold me in peace.

Light fades here as it does
elsewhere, but with
more effect,
the vast stretch of sea
reaching for France
loses reflections slowly,
sinks back
to silence, stippled with
moving patterns.

Fortuneswell Under Snow

Seen for the first time under snow
the particular magic of this place
grows a new face,
rough contours of the cliff
softened beneath a gathering of flakes.

Blue-grey expanse of sea provides
a darkening background
to the tangled roofs,
where lightly frosted chimney pots,
pointing with cheeky gestures to the sky,
rise above layers of crystal
crunching beneath the feet of startled gulls.

Indoors, new harmony of composition:
a distant swelling on the harp
but mostly in words
softer than yesterday's,
opposing melodies now coming together,
a covering as gentle as the snow.

No-One at Home

(for Kay Cotton)

Touching and sniffing
I walk warily round,
as a child left alone
in an empty house
full of adult things
tries on mothers rings,
a squirt of her scent.

I wash off the journey
with Vetiver soap,
see my face in your glass
and finger your amber,
the necklace I gave you
still smelling of you,
Mitsouko close by.

Enviously counting
fruit on your orange tree
I stop at twenty-three –
mine only has blossom –
nervously smoothing
soft peacock feathers
I fear on my face.

Delightedly stroking
the pert yellow duck,
the driftwood stuck
on the bathroom door,
your hat on a hook,
a pot of geraniums
bright in the bidet.

Ignoring temptation –
the unicorn on the divan –
I flop in the chair
ready placed at your desk
and plot out the course
for better or worse
of this whimsical verse.

Valentine Birthday

(for Scottie, still.)

It wasn't that I wanted to be rid
of the responsibility, or that
I loved you less for being
a little silly;
I just needed to know where we stood
and how to get help when things
got worse, as I feared
they would.

So we went along to the hospital to
see the appropriate specialist.
You went in trustingly,
"a nice old man",
you said when you came out.
I went in after you; glad that he
hadn't alarmed you, as I had
feared he might.

"Oh yes, she's dementing", he began,
"can't even remember her birthday".
"Neither might you," I snapped
"if you were illegitimate, and your mother had
dumped you, aged three, sailing off
to Canada with her sister, leaving
you behind."

"Chocolates and a Valentine card
every year on her birthday,
February 14th, an ironic
coincidence.
She shared the chocolates with me,
bitter in my mouth, as the censure
I couldn't even express when I finally
met her mother."

"No," he explained, "it's the last thing
they forget," passed me a tissue,
gave me some useful advice, and
saw me out.
So we went home together, I trying to
forget that nothing would ever be
the same again, you, looking
forward to tea.

Journey into Day

For me each morning is a difficult birth,
a pulling from the womb of my embryo self,
a hurting process and the beginning
of a journey that has no purpose
no sense of direction and no obligation
to follow through, carve out a pattern
or make a shining thing of each new day.

Energy seeps slowly over my consciousness,
day bumbles on after the midwife's strictures,
her admonishing and irritating advice
about feeding and nurturing
and letting things take their natural course.
There is nothing natural about morning –
each day is my child
to be strangled at birth if that is what I want!

Only once have I felt differently,
after a totally sleepless night
spent hugging my happiness
tightly as a hot-water bottle,
crowing for joy when the dawn rang my curtains back
and the day with its promise of you could begin.

Switching the Sun

It's not just from proper sleep at night
that I wake with a sense of loss,
conscious of companionship
rudely snatched.

Nor from the catnaps
that some people find refreshing,
but from great swathes of sleep:
mornings, afternoons, evenings
in my chair,
waking to my coffee cold,
and always that disturbing sense
of a presence
hurriedly withdrawn.

The consolation of a dream
can be worse:
I hear my sister's pungent wit,
her use of irony to underline her meaning;
I listen till I find myself speaking in the same tone
her words coming from my lips,
then I wake to my voice
in the empty room.

Friends who visit me in the afternoon
can be disconcerting too;
we chat
of this and that,
exchange snippets of gossip and local news,
then suddenly they fade backwards through the wall,
leaving me awkward
and amazed.

Most people talk to me kindly
assuming that I need to be reassured,
to have my problems solved from the outside,
though when I try to say

it is not a problem
but a sense of isolation,
they put that down to self-pity.

Some friends still switch the sun on
when they walk into a room,
but they have taken their magic to a far place
and I cannot always reach them.
I know now what my mother meant
when she said I could be lonely
if I did not marry.

2.

Emptiness
is not the same as loneliness
rather a loss of self,
of the prevalence of thought,
the word that used to sustain.
Depression
is not just a weight of misery:
it robs the mind of conviction,
the ability to make decisions,
and leaves one floundering
in a sea of infantile questions.

Fearfully
I look for the first sign of senility:
is it just forgetting the order of things
or losing a valid sense of order,
the structure that once held things together –
forgetting how to communicate?
My head spins
my feet skid,
I hold onto myself, struggle for control.

The clouded vision that is all I see
must clear someday,
the buzzing in my ears
subside;
light will irradiate the darkness,

darkness
fade into memory.
It has happened before
and will happen again.

My cast of mind – inherited –
makes the transition difficult,
but once more surrounded by light,
eyes focussed on truth,
capacity for listening
restored,
I will know my life of value
and find my place in the pattern again.

Not Pandora's Box, but Mine

(for Sian Morris)

At last I feel the weight
lifting a little,
the box of my depression
has a looser lid,
that leaves a small crack
through which I can breathe out
some of the stale air
and breathe in a freshness
that smells faintly of lavender.

A friend told me recently
she was going
to Lourdes, not in any hope of a cure
but because it is a way
she can travel and be looked after,
see new places
in the company of interesting people.
So wise of her
not to expect a personal miracle.

Months of introspection
have left me
heavy with pain and weariness
and aware that for me, too,
there will be
no miracle. Still I wake
tentatively, hopeful that ten pills
and a little exercise later
I will be almost ready to face the day.

And the day when it comes
ticks over slowly,
not the accustomed drag.
I walk into the garden
in which Adam is taking such an interest,
and see with new eyes the plants
that he has freed from
their surrounding weeds, and
dead-head my Heartsease carefully.

Palea Epidavros

(for Gil Rosen)

Hiding behind a solid wall of cloud
the sun gathers itself for rising, proud
to send exploring fingers tipped with light
to sweep the mountain tops, erasing night.

Stone walls around the villas seem to brood:
walls are important here, some have withstood
conflict of centuries, long search for truth,
ancient philosophy, studied still by youth.

Some years ago we saw the first few stones
uncovered from dark layers of time, the bones
of history; now, tiers of seats revealed,
a second theatre rises in rough field.

Full moon in the night sky, round crimson sun,
glory of day that never is quite done;
high on the mountain road among the goats
gift in such measure catches at the throat.

Feeding Time at Caffe Neros

They land like a flock of birds twittering on my garden table,
– glossy hedge sparrows, blue tits, and a red-splashed robin –
devour chunks of Italian bread and paninis thrown, peck
at the window glass: cheesecakes, gateau, chocolate brownies,
choices temptingly displayed, all of them there for the picking.

Once fed, they linger at the tables, drink their espresso, shout
cheerfully to each other, still reminding me of colourful birds.
I watch as they preen their feathers, smooth them down again,
reckon them not long out of the nest, missing titbits from Mum,
stretching their wings and trying on new personalities for size.

Happy with their choice, they wear their brightest plumage,
voice controversial topics as loudly as they like, try out
new theories, throw arguments around, toss conversations
to the ceiling lights, catch them descending, hold the noise level,
order more coffee and begin again, unconscious of my stare.

Women on Women

(for U.A.Fanthorpe and, of course, for Rosie too.)

Collecteds are not meant
to be read right through
at a sitting, or two,
even when one knows them
already from the component parts
and is looking mostly for loved lines
to cheer, to hearten or console.

But yours, as ever, is different
and is sometimes to be read as I did
this afternoon, in one huge gobble,
ostensibly for reference:
to find a poem about one woman
explaining in its cleverness
all there is to be known about her.

Of course I didn't find one, not one
that could be isolated to imply
love of the entire breadth
of womanliness. Instead
I found comprehension and love
of woman in all her guises,
and especially one.

Perhaps
it will be possible to include
them all in this anthology
that is intended to feature only
poems by women poets,
and especially the best of them.
Yours would light up the pages
with knowledge and understanding,
with humour and tenderness
and leave me weeping
as I did this afternoon.

The Artist's Model

(for Chris and Sue Tisdall)

Framed by my window, an artist stands
in the churchyard sketching a young girl.
She sits easily on a straight-backed chair
wearing a 1920's picture hat, her skirt
falling in soft folds to her feet. As I watch
she shifts her position, shifts it again
and smiles placatingly at her tormentor.

A masterpiece in the making? Am I seeing
some yet to be discovered Monet forsaking
his water lilies for our unkempt grass
untidy hedge and bushed-out lime trees,
the old stone church discreetly to one side.
Will it be famous one day as portrait of Alice
the unknown model who was also his mistress?

She stands up suddenly, pushes her hands
under her hat and into her hair. I imagine her
saying 'Come on Archie, I've had enough?'
But he, taking advantage of her movement,
turns round to sketch my cottage instead.
I'm used to that, but perhaps this one will be
different, famous for being in his portfolio.

Later they both get to their feet, gather their
assorted belongings, folding chair, camera,
sketching gear in a disillusioning Sainsbury's
carrier bag, and move on out of my vision.
Something about their walk arrests my eye
but I refuse to admit that I might know them:
that would dispel my moment of history.

Shrinkage

Two children measuring themselves
against each other –
how long since I stood tall
to chalk marks on the wall,
passing my sister's level, proud to be
the tall one in the family?

Grown up, my sister viewed my kitchen
wistfully: *if I were as tall as you*,
she said, *I could keep my saucepans*
on a high shelf. Now, Janet dead,
the years have shrunk me
till my pride of height is but a bent old woman.

My saucepans, banished to the back porch,
are well within my reach,
cupboards stacked to the front
where I do not have to bend,
and kitchen chores
carried out sitting safely on a stool.

I resent it all, (not being old, that just
happens), read the *Guardian*
flinching at most of the news, sit
with the easy crossword to my coffee, write
angry letters in my head
and still the occasional angry poem.

Perception

(for Kevin Crossley-Holland)

You gave me back myself,
seeing right through the layers of age and pain
to find the woman who was always there,

the knack you always had –
seeing the best and worst in everyone
and skirting round the desert in between,

that hint of coquetry
you can't subdue and would not if you could,
the glint of youth still shining in your eyes.

We talked of this and that
of people loved and not loved in the past,
so many blessedly still here for us;

talked, too, of poetry,
of principles on which we both agree
and other issues that we both dispute.

I found some wine to pour,
fretting at frugal hospitality,
explaining I had tried to bake rock buns;

you gathered up the crumbs
and picked them off the plate – the biscuits that
my would-be cakes had sadly shrivelled to.

You said you felt at home,
so that again these walls held home for me
not just enclosing disability.

D-Day Comes Alive

Why are my memories not clear like theirs –
those veterans who march in step and joke
about their time together in the war,
how bravely men survived with limbs blown off,
how well their comrades fought before they died.

Brushes with death, miraculous escapes,
the unexploded bombs, bullets misfired –
their recollections are of danger faced,
of duty carried to the mouth of hell
by boys of seventeen too young to die.

It is the camaraderie they had
that lingers in the mind, both theirs and mine,
and colours all their memories with gold
as they relive a time when boys were men
and shared excitement held them as a bond.

For me it was a new experience
living alongside men who knew so much
about the possibility of death,
who'd all been to the edge and back again
and learned to pass it off as commonplace.

Imprisoned in the grounds of Exbury House,
we knew so little of the outside world,
of silent preparations for the war;
we only knew that all our leave was stopped
and were not told the reason, left to guess.

Earning my buttons, moved to Portsdown Hill,
responsible for Wrens with fearsome bikes
delivering despatches urgently
to ships in Portsmouth Dock, and back again,
I moved a little closer to the scene.

Noisy and difficult they needed space
to let off steam from tensions of the day,
unwinding as they settled in their bunks,
as I walked to Fort Southwick through the dark
to make ship's cocoa for the early watch.

So now that sixty years have come and gone
I watch the celebrations with unease;
could I have known so little, felt so much,
cared deeply in that heightened atmosphere
to wait till now to know that I was there.

Living it up in my Eighties

When I was a girl we wore liberty bodices, not bras,
designed to conceal rather than reveal
the embarrassment of curves;
liberty was a misnomer.

Then came the corselette, a full-length garment
only less constricting than a strait-jacket,
designed, I suppose, to keep us
strictly inaccessible.

Today, I am shocked by teenagers: nipples on show
through everyday wear, flesh boldly revealed
between skimpy tops and jeans, gold rings
in pierced navels.

I, like everyone my age, am decently covered,
wearing a respectable bra, but otherwise
comfortably uncorseted, free to move
in any direction.

How I enjoy driving my invalid scooter on the pavement,
scattering the groups of half-clad teenagers –
loitering there without purpose –
with unseemly glee.

They regard me with a certain amused disdain, which
bothers me not at all as I drive erratically on –
maximum four miles an hour –
in my out-of-date gear.

Little do they know! Still a teenager at heart, I revel in now,
confounding convention, surrounding myself with
admiring young men, and living it up
in my eighties.